When **Sally** Met **Scrum**

Experience the Scrum Guide through a captivating story.

Manav Agarwal

Copyright © 2024 Manav Agarwal

All rights reserved.

ISBN: 9798338738535

Dedication

For the countless people who have been part of my agile journey:

For the participants of my Agile workshops and courses, whose insightful questions and unique challenges from different teams, industries, and sectors have deepened and shaped my understanding of Scrum time and time again. Your curiosity and real-world scenarios have led me to find creative ways to implement Scrum in a wide variety of settings and breathe life into the framework, far beyond the pages of the Scrum Guide.

For all the Scrum teams that I have been able to accompany in various roles - as Agile Coach, Product Owner,r or Scrum Master. Every project, every sprint and every event was another step on my personal and professional development journey. Your successes, your challenges, and your relentless pursuit of continuous improvement have been my greatest teachers.

For my clients, whose trust and encouragement have given me wings. Your willingness to embrace change and your enthusiasm to transform your work environments towards Scrum and Agile have been both inspiring and humbling. This book is a testament to your courage and vision.

And finally, for every "Sally" out there - the changemakers, the questioners, the innovators in organizations large and small. May this book inspire you to start your agile revolutions - one sprint at a time.

Contents

A Day in BA Paradise   1

Operation Odyssey Begins   9

Odyssey in Stormy Waters   15

"Agile" Chaos   23

The Secret Scrum   33

Scrum in Secret   43

Deeper into the Scrum Waters   53

The Big Scrum Coming Out   63

Scrum Comes of Age   73

ACKNOWLEDGMENT

This book is the result of countless interactions, experiences, and insights I've gained through an incredible community of Agile practitioners and enthusiasts.

First of all, my heartfelt thanks go to all the participants in my Agile workshops and courses. Your questions, arising from the unique challenges of your teams and industries, have been the cornerstone of my growing understanding of Scrum. Whether in healthcare, finance, public administration, or start-ups, your diverse perspectives have led me to explore the versatility of Scrum and find new, innovative ways to apply it in different areas. You are the co-creators of this book and have shaped it with every question like "But how does it work in our industry?".

A huge thank you goes out to all the Scrum teams I have had the honor of working with. As an Agile Coach, Product Owner, and Scrum Master, I have been lucky enough to be part of your journeys. Every sprint planning, every daily standup, every review, and every retrospective added a new dimension to my Scrum knowledge. Your successes have been my successes, your challenges my learning moments. This book is as much a product of your experiences as my words.

To my customers who dared to embark on the path of agile transformation with me - your trust was my greatest motivation. Your willingness to question the status quo, embrace change, and relentlessly strive for improvement has been an inexhaustible source of inspiration. The stories in this book reflect your courage and determination.

A very special thank you to my family and friends who patiently endured my endless scrum analogies daily and supported me through the ups and downs of the writing process. Your love and encouragement were my constant sprint goal.

Finally, I would like to thank you, the reader. By choosing to pick up this book, you are taking a step towards better understanding and applying Scrum. Whether you are a Scrum novice or an experienced Agile practitioner, I hope Sally's story speaks to you and enriches your Scrum journey.

Remember, as the Scrum Guide says, "Scrum is free and offered in this guide." This book is merely a fun way to experience it - a way that has been shaped by the accumulated knowledge of countless Agile practitioners. May your sprints be productive, your backlogs well-maintained and your retrospectives insightful!

Thank you all for being part of this incredible Agile journey. This book was created for you and because of you.

Chapter 1

A Day in BA Paradise

There I was, Sally McKinnon, living my over-caffeinated, sticky-note-filled life as a Business Analyst. On this particular day – which could have been Tuesday or Wednesday, honestly, who remembers anymore? – chaos was my constant companion.

Oh, the joys of the BA life...

7:00 am: Get up and shine

or at least get up

My alarm clock plays the tune from "Mission Impossible". How appropriate. I turn lazily to the other side, reach for my smartphone, and start scrolling through the barrage of e-mails.

Three new meeting requests, two "urgent" matters, and a wildcard - it looks like I have to fight my way through this day like a mole through concrete.

In a perfect world, I would start my day with yoga or meditation. But who am I trying to fool here? My inner peace only comes from a cup of coffee, black as my soul after a day of meetings.

8:30 am: Entrance to the Matrix

aka the office

With my laptop in one hand and a huge coffee in the other—my shield and my weapon—I stride boldly into the office. Imagine an office crammed with process diagrams that look like abstract art, scenarios that would make Kafka green with envy, and a never-ending stream of stakeholders.

My colleague Dave, who I secretly call "The Developer" (as if it were his superhero alias), grunts a "Wassup?". Maybe he needs a cup of coffee. It's always a thing with developers - you never know whether a grunt means "Good morning" or "I've just coded the apocalypse".

9:00 a.m.: The daily stand-up

aka "speed dating for project updates"

By 9, our team leader Linda, armed with a smile probably powered by too much espresso, opens the stand-up. "Okay, guys, quick round - who did what yesterday, what are you doing today and are there any obstacles?"

Quick? Ha! I've seen glaciers melt faster than these "short" updates. It's like trying to summarize "War and Peace" in a tweet. My turn came and I put on my best "everything is fine" face and continued.

"Yesterday I completed all the backend processes for the new payment gateway. Today, I'll meet the UX team to create the wireframes and I'm updating our backlog. No problems in sight, except we're finally trying to figure out who's stealing all my good pens every week."

I reached into my drawer, pulled out a cheap, plastic ballpoint pen with a corporate logo chewed off the end, and clicked it a few times. This will have to do. The good ones were staying hidden today.

10:30 a.m.: Customer meeting

"The Wish-Hunger Games"

An hour and a half later, I found myself with Brad, our main customer from marketing, inside the conference room. Supposedly to get started in defining the specifications for the new landing page.

The glint in his eyes was something that I was familiar with yet afraid of. And the knot in my stomach tightened when he finally said, "You know, Sally," eyes twinkling with confidence, "last night I had an idea. What if we make the site more interactive?"

More interactive? Last week, you wanted "simple and minimalist". I swear, Brad's opinion changes faster than the weather in London.

"Interesting, Brad. Let's look at some options. But before we do, could you remind me what the main goals of the site are?"

That's his cue to launch into a monologue about engagement metrics and branding. I doodle his vision dreamily on the whiteboard. By the end, we have a diagram that looks like a cross between a flowchart and an abstract painting.

1:00 pm: Lunch

if you can call it that

Lunch came and I found myself unwrapping my sad sandwich with one hand at my desk while scrolling through emails with the other. Multitasking at its finest. I was dreaming of a real lunch break, I would go higher and dream of maybe even stepping outside to breathe fresh air, but my dreams were cut short when Dave poked his head over our office wall like a curious groundhog.

"Hey Sally, a quick question about the user story for the password reset function..."

Well, that was it for lunch. At least I managed two bites.

6:27 pm: "Closing time"

haha!

After launching our project management tool and moving tasks back and forth, adding notes and asking Dave for time estimates, I quickly answer a few "just a quick question" emails and put together the to-do list for tomorrow. It's like trying to divert a river with a teaspoon.

You know it's getting serious when your to-do list itself needs a to-do list.

When I finally shut down my computer and grab my bag, I make the rookie mistake of taking a quick look at my phone. Three new emails, a Slack message, and a calendar invitation for a meeting at 7 am.

Sigh. Wonderful. Did I mention that I'm not a morning person?

9:15 p.m.: "Me-Time"

"Still at work in your head"

I'm in my evening yoga class and have twisted into a position that I'm pretty sure is anatomically impossible and not in any yoga book. Suddenly it hits me - the perfect solution to our payment gateway problem!

Must... resist... the urge... to check... emails.

As I try to focus on my breathing instead of API integrations (spoiler: it's not working), I can't help but think: there must be a better way to manage all this, right? A... more agile approach perhaps?

What I didn't know at the time was that my world was about to change completely. And you would soon find out why.

Manav's Thoughts

Reading Sally's story reminds me of countless teams I've worked with over the past decade. What we see here is a classic example of a broken system, not broken people. Let me share what stands out from this chapter.

Sally's day represents what I call the "*chaos carousel*" - a constant stream of interruptions, urgent requests, and context switching. In my experience coaching teams across different industries, this pattern is remarkably common and consistently destructive to both productivity and well-being.

The daily stand-up meeting they have is particularly interesting. They've adopted the practice of having a daily meeting, but it's become this lengthy status update that adds to their problems rather than solving them. I've seen this countless times - teams adopt certain practices without understanding their purpose, turning potentially valuable tools into time-wasting ceremonies.

Brad from Marketing represents a challenge I've encountered in almost every organization - the "idea fountain." It's not that his ideas are bad, but there's no structured way to handle changes and new requirements. The team simply absorbs everything thrown at them, leading to constant disruption and unclear priorities.

What resonates with me is how Sally tries to solve these problems. More documentation, longer hours, working through lunch - these are all symptoms of trying to solve tomorrow's problems with yesterday's tools. Many talented professionals who use this approach eventually burn out.

The most telling moment comes during Sally's yoga class. That thought - "there must be a better way" - is often the catalyst for change. In my years of coaching teams through transformation,

I've learned to look for these moments. When people start questioning the status quo, that's when real improvement becomes possible.

This chapter essentially shows us what happens when we try to manage modern business complexity with traditional approaches. We see a dedicated professional doing their best within a system that's setting them up for frustration. The constant interruptions, the never-ending documentation, the reactive nature of work - these aren't personal failures, they're system failures.

But here's what gives me hope: every challenge we see in Sally's day is solvable. Not through more documentation or longer hours, but through better ways of working together. The problems are clear - now, it's time to explore the solutions.

Chapter 2

Operation Odyssey Begins

How I learned to love chaos

Remember when I said my world was about to turn upside down? Well, you're about to find out why. Fasten your seatbelts and hold on tight, because we're setting sail on Operation Odyssey.

A ship that has more leaks than the Titanic.

The big announcement

The day we were too happy

Our CEO Karen stands in front of everyone, we are in an "all-hands" meeting where the coffee is fresher than the ideas and the atmosphere is more charged than a lightning during a thunderstorm.

"Team," Karen announces with a smile brighter than the sun, "this is our moment! Operation Odyssey will revolutionize how people manage their finances!"

Super. No pressure. It's just about revolutionizing the entire personal finance system. Maybe later we'll also solve climate change and find a diet where you can eat bacon every day and still lose weight.

I let my gaze wander around the room. Dave, the developer, is awake for once. Linda, our team leader, is scribbling so vigorously in her notebook that I fear she might rip the paper. And Brad from Marketing? He's vibrating with enthusiasm, like a bee buzzing around.

Karen continues: "Let's start the detailed project planning right away!"

Ah yes, the battle cry of every innovation: "We've always done it this way!" Why change something when you can keep tripping over the same stone?

The planning phase

"Death by a thousand spreadsheets"

Cut to two weeks later. I'm buried under a mountain of "requirements documents" taller than the Burj Khalifa. My desk looks like a paper factory and I think I've developed an allergy to Post-its.

Dave looks over the wall of our shared office, his eyes wide with tension and probably caffeine. "Hey Sally, how's it going with the requirements document? We need to start development... um... *yesterday*."

"Almost done, Dave. I'm just finalizing the last details with Brad." I reply. *Finalizing as in feeling like I'm nailing pudding into the wall.*

"Cool, cool," Dave nods, obviously lost in thought. "Remember, the requirements have to be complete before we write a single line of code. No more changes once we've started!"

Absolutely complete? Sure, and maybe pigs will fly at the same time stakeholders will stop having "brilliant" ideas in the shower.

The Gantt chart

that beats all Gantt charts

Linda calls me into her office. A colorful chaos that she proudly presents as a project plan projected on a screen. A rainbow kaleidoscope.

"Sally, can you check the schedule?" asks Linda, pointing at the screen. "I've detailed every task, subtask, and sub-sub-task for the next 18 months."

I squint my eyes and try to decipher the rainbow mayhem in front of me. It's like trying to find a specific item in a hyper-organized but overstuffed junk drawer—everything has a place, but good luck figuring it out.

"Wow, Linda, that's... comprehensive."

If "comprehensive" means something like "completely out of touch with reality and probably already out of date before we leave the room".

"I know, right? Isn't it beautiful?" enthuses Linda. "Look, I've even planned for potential sick days and software updates!"

I wonder if she has also planned for the inevitable breakdowns of doing this plan. Maybe we should schedule group therapy sessions as well.

"It's definitely... something special," I replied diplomatically.

The requirements document

from hell

Back at my desk, I put the finishing touches to the 200-page monster that is our requirements documents. Brad comes sauntering up with that mischievous glint in his eye that I dread.

"Sally, I had a brilliant idea while jogging this morning. What if we built a virtual financial advisor avatar into the app? Just like Siri, only for money!"

An idea, he says. The only idea I have right now is how I can teleport myself to a tropical island without Wi-Fi. Maybe there I'll finally find the work-life balance that everyone talks about but no one has ever seen.

"That's... an interesting idea, Brad," I say, trying to keep the panic out of my voice. "But we're about to finalize the requirements. Adding something this big now would-"

"Oh, it'll be fine!" Brad waves it off with a carefree attitude. "Just squeeze it in somewhere. I'm sure the developers won't mind!"

As Brad trundles off, I stare at the screen. The requirements document now feels both frighteningly incomplete and overwhelmingly complex. It's like a puzzle with half the pieces missing and the other half not fitting together.

There must be a better way. A way that doesn't involve writing a novel-length requirements document that is out of date before the ink is dry. A way that is more adaptable than a chameleon and more efficient than an Oktoberfest waiter.

Manav's Thoughts

This chapter powerfully illustrates what I call "waterfall wishful thinking" - a phenomenon I've seen multiple times in traditional organizations that are attempting large transformations. Let me tell you what stands out.

The all-hands meeting scene perfectly captures how transformational projects often begin - with grand visions but traditional execution mindsets. Karen's announcement of Operation Odyssey shows a common disconnect: big ambitions paired with old-school planning methods. This approach repeatedly leads to project failures.

The "comprehensive requirements" mindset displayed here is particularly problematic. Dave's insistence that requirements must be complete before coding begins, and Linda's 18-month Gantt chart, represent the "perfect plan fallacy." In my experience coaching teams, this approach consistently fails because it assumes we can predict both the problems and their solutions in advance.

Brad's last-minute feature request - the financial advisor avatar - exemplifies another common challenge: the inability to handle change. In traditional project management, changes are seen as disruptions to be resisted rather than opportunities to be embraced. I've been a witness to countless teams struggling with this tension between fixed plans and evolving requirements.

What's striking is how everyone knows the approach isn't working, yet they persist with it. Sally's metaphor of "nailing pudding to the wall" perfectly describes what many teams go through when trying to define everything upfront. This pattern repeats across industries, such as financial institutions, tech companies, and manufacturing firms.

The 200-page requirements document represents the "documentation theater" - creating comprehensive documents that provide an illusion of control but slow down value delivery. In my years of coaching, I've never seen such documents successfully guide a project to completion.

The chapter ends with an apt prediction about these plans meeting reality. After working with hundreds of teams, I can confirm that detailed upfront planning for complex projects doesn't work out. The question isn't if the plan will change, but how we manage when it does.

Chapter 3

Odyssey in Stormy Waters

When reality torpedoes your plans

After almost drowning in a sea of documents and clinging to the 200-page requirements manifesto for dear life. Let's see what happens when Operation Odyssey hits the high seas of development.

Spoiler: It's going to be a stormy ride.

The development kickoff

"The last day of blissful ignorance"

The air in the assembly room was so thick with the scent of whiteboard markers and misguided optimism that you could cut it with a knife. Our development team is assembled and looking at me expectantly.

"All right, team," I begin, heaving the request document onto the table with a thud that sounds like I've just dropped the New York phone book. "Here's everything you need to know about Operation Odyssey."

Dave eyes the document suspiciously. "Everything, yeah? Are you sure you haven't forgotten anything? Maybe the kitchen and sink and the recycling center as well?"

Oh, Dave. If only you knew about the virtual financial advisor avatar.

I start my presentation and walk them through user stories, flowcharts, and enough user cases to send even the most caffeinated developer into a state of unconsciousness. Two hours later, I finish, my voice hoarse from the endless monologuing.

"So, any questions?"

The room is so quiet that you could have heard a pin drop. Then, from behind, a shy voice: "Can you explain the whole thing again, but this time in easy English?"

I suppress the impulse to bang my head rhythmically against the wall. Sigh. It's going to be a longer project than the construction work on the Great Wall of China.

The first month

"Calm seas... or so we thought"

In the first few weeks, everything seems to be going according to plan. The developers are busy programming away. Linda's Gantt chart is still mostly green, calming as an alpine meadow in spring. And me? I answer the usual flood of questions and clarifications like a human ChatGPT.

I swing by Dave's desk for our daily check-in, armed with a coffee strong enough to wake the dead. "How's it going? Good progress?"

Dave looks up, his eyes slightly manic. "Oh yeah, great progress. We're only, well, about 73 user stories behind schedule. But who's counting, right?"

I'm counting, Dave. I count. And Linda too, and Karen, and probably every single shareholder in our company.

"Well, I'm sure you'll catch up," I say, trying to put some optimism into my voice.

"Is there anything I can do to help?"

Dave laughs. Not a happy laugh but a derisive one, the life seemingly lost in his eyes. "Unless you can pack more hours into the day or make sure those requirements no longer conflict, I think we're good to go."

Conflicting requirements? Impossible. My document is perfect. It says so on page 147, subsection B, paragraph 3. *Maybe I should have it carved in stone to make it even more binding.*

The stakeholder meeting

"The day the music died"

About two months later, we had our first big stakeholder review. Karen, Brad, and some board members are gathered to see our progress. The atmosphere is as tense as a courtroom during a OJ Simpson trial.

Dave begins his demo, his finger hovering nervously over the mouse. "So, as you can see, if you click here-"

"Wait a minute," Brad interrupts, his forehead creased. "Why is this button blue? It should be green. Green goes down better with millennials."

Oh no. No, no, no. Don't do this, Brad. Not now. Not after all those night shifts and coffee overdoses.

Dave looks at me, panic in his eyes like a deer in headlights. I cut in, my voice as calm as possible, "Now, Brad, according to the requirements document, section 72, subsection F-"

"Requisition document?" Brad waves defensively as if shooing away an annoying fly. "That old thing? We're beyond that. Stay on the ball, Sally!"

Beyond that? BEYOND THAT? This "old thing" is my magnum opus, my Mona Lisa of requirements documentation!

Karen clears her throat, like a rumble of an approaching thunderstorm. "Maybe we could focus on functionality? Dave, please go ahead."

Dave nods, visibly relieved, and clicks to the next screen. "And this is where users can set their savings goals-"

"Savings goals?" This time Karen interrupts, her voice sharp with a knife-like quality. "I thought we were talking about budgeting. Why are we talking about saving money?"

Because it's in the requirements, Karen. The requirements that YOU signed off on. The ones I've had tattooed on my eyelids for three months that I could recite them in my sleep.

As the room descends into chaos, with stakeholders arguing about features, colors, and fonts (fonts!), I sink deeper into my chair.

There must be a better way. A way for all of this to work, a way where we don't throw away our plans as soon as we finalize them. There has to.

The aftermath

"Rearranging deckchairs on the Titanic"

The now irrelevant requirements document stares at me back at my desk. I dreamily imagine myself throwing it into the dumpster fire that our project has become. Or maybe I could fold it into a thousand origami cranes so I can wish for our project to work.

Linda emerges, left eye twitching slightly. "Sally, we need to update the project plan. And by 'update' I mean completely revise, possibly while screaming into a pillow."

I nod, beyond words at this point. *I feel like a hamster in a wheel that has just realized it has nowhere to go.*

"Oh, and Karen wants us to be more 'agile,'" Linda continues, making quotation marks in the air.

Agile. I've heard this term before. It's supposed to be the solution to all our problems, right? The project management equivalent of sliced bread. Or maybe more like whole wheat bread - everyone says it's good for you, but no one knows why.

"So what does that mean for us?" I ask with fear.

Linda's smile is slightly manic as if she's just got hold of the last drop of coffee in the office. "Oh, you know. We'll have daily stand-up meetings, and sticky notes on a whiteboard and call it all a 'sprint'. That'll solve everything, right?"

That's right. Because renaming things always solves deep-seated process problems. Why didn't we think of this earlier? Maybe we should also call our bugs "unplanned features" and hope they go away on their own.

As Linda walks away muttering to herself about burndown charts and velocity, terms that sound as if from a foreign language, I turn back to my computer. I open a new browser tab and type with the desperation of a drowning man reaching for a life preserver.

"What the hell is Agile anyway?"

Little did I know that this innocent Google search would lead me down a rabbit hole deeper than the Mariana Trench and change my life more than the invention of the doner kebab. But that is a story for our next chapter.

Manav's Thoughts

This chapter vividly illustrates what happens when traditional project management meets reality—a collision. The development kickoff scene, with Sally presenting her massive requirements document, perfectly captures a moment I've seen replay across different organizations: the illusion of completeness colliding with the reality of software development.

The "calm seas" period in the first month is telling. Teams appear to make progress initially, but they're often building on shifting sands. Dave's revelation about being 73 user stories behind schedule isn't just about falling behind - it's about the fundamental mismatch between fixed plans and the reality of complex projects.

The stakeholder review scene resonates deeply with my experience. The debate about button colors and the dismissal of the requirements document as "that old thing" highlights a critical problem: the disconnect between upfront planning and evolving business needs. When Brad casually suggests ignoring the requirements document, he's unknowingly pointing out a fundamental flaw in traditional project management—the assumption that requirements can be frozen in time.

Karen's reaction to the savings goals versus budgeting feature mirrors a situation I had with a banking client. Leadership had signed off on detailed requirements but had different expectations when seeing the actual product. Stakeholders often don't fully grasp the implications of written requirements until they see working software.

Meanwhile, the aftermath section shows the desperation that often precedes transformation. Linda's suggestion to become more "agile" by simply adopting ceremonies like daily stand-ups and sticky notes represents how organizations often try to adopt agile practices superficially without understanding the underlying principles.

Sally's final move - turning to Google to understand Agile - is a pivotal moment, representing the crucial point where professionals realize there must be a better way. The frustration with current processes becomes a catalyst for genuine change.

This chapter represents a critical turning point: the moment when the traditional approach definitively fails, creating an opening for real transformation. It's not just about the failure of a single project—it's about the collective realization that the entire approach to building software needs to change.

Chapter 4

"Agile" Chaos

How I stopped worrying and learned to love sticky note

In hopes of finding what Agile means, who would've thought that the answer was just a few types away? Little did I know that this discovery would be hindered by a huge roadblock made of sticky notes.

The midnight oil burn

It's 2 AM, and here I am, still at my desk, bathed in the pale light of my computer screen. I've fallen through an internet rabbit hole reading about this thing called *"Scrum."* My coffee is stone-cold, my eyes feel like they've turned into sandpaper, and the concept of daylight feels like a distant memory. Still, I can't stop reading.

Scrum. At first glance, it sounded like rugby—a bit of pushing, shoving, and maybe tackling problems head-on. I even chuckled at the idea of building a human pyramid of developers to carry our software over the finish line. But as I delved deeper, I realized it was much more than sticky notes and endless meetings.

Scrum is about something bigger—*value creation*. That phrase stopped me in my tracks. It's not just about checking off tasks or hitting arbitrary deadlines. It's about ensuring that everything we do—every sprint, every backlog item—produces something meaningful. It's about delivering results that matter to the people who use our work and to the business goals we're trying to achieve.

This idea of value creation felt both revolutionary and oddly simple. I glanced at the mountain of requirements documents stacked on my desk, their purpose suddenly feeling hollow.

Have these documents ever delivered real value to anyone? Or have they just kept the paper industry afloat?

Scrum shifts the focus entirely: instead of obsessing over rigid processes, it encourages collaboration, adaptability, and constant re-evaluation of what truly matters. It's about asking, *"Are we solving the right problem? Are we delivering something useful?"* rather than just blindly following a plan.

The more I read, the clearer it became: Scrum isn't just a framework—it's a mindset.

A commitment to doing work that has purpose, impact, and meaning. And maybe, just maybe, that's what my work has been missing all along.

The Scrum Guide enlightenment

Just when I thought I'd reached the end of my internet journey, I stumbled across something called "The Scrum Guide". It's short, simple, and... makes sense? I blink rapidly and wonder if I'm hallucinating from all the coffee I've consumed or if this is coherent.

Wait a minute, there are rules to this Agile thing? It's not just about renaming all our meetings to make them sound cooler.

I feel like I've discovered the holy grail of project management, complete with a handy PDF format. As if I've been given a map after walking in an endless maze for months on end.

As I dive into the guide, I'm impressed by its accessibility. It's free, available online, and written in language that doesn't require a PhD in buzzwordology. *I should send a thank you card to the authors Ken Schwaber and Jeff Sutherland.*

As I continue, I'm introduced to *sprints*. These aren't marathons where we burn out midway—they're neat, timeboxed intervals where work happens, progress is inspected, and plans adapt. Each sprint is like a Russian Matryoshka doll: daily scrums, product backlogs, and increments are all neatly nested inside.

I imagine a tiny Scrum Master cheerfully overseeing miniature planning sessions, and I chuckle to myself. Maybe I need more coffee. Or less?

Then comes the "Definition of Done". It's not just that blissful state you achieve after clearing your inbox or surviving the Monday morning meeting. Nope, it's a real, transparent checklist used to determine whether a product increment is complete. A practical guide for perfectionists—and it's helpful. Unlike my personal to-do list, which still includes "survive" and "drink more coffee".

What makes my sleep-deprived brain sit up, though, is the concept of empirical process control. Scrum isn't just organized chaos; it's grounded in the three pillars: *transparency, inspection, and adaptation.* It's like the project management version of "see, hear, act," but instead of sweeping problems under the rug, you face them head-on with a magnifying glass and a plan. Transparency lets everyone see what's happening, inspection ensures you're on track, and adaptation... well, that's the secret sauce to staying afloat when things inevitably go sideways.

As I read, I feel a spark of hope ignite in my chest. *This could be the answer to our Operation Odyssey problems. We could actually finish something in a reasonable timeframe, get feedback before we've built the whole thing, and maybe, just maybe, stop drowning in a sea of outdated requirements.*

Goodbye, Documentation

The next day, Karen, our eternally optimistic managing director, gathered us all in the conference room again. Her smile is so radiant that I wonder if she has been secretly eating light bulbs.

"Team," she announces with the enthusiasm of a child who has just learned that Christmas is happening twice this year, "I had an epiphany. We need to become more agile!"

Oh dear, here we go. I can already feel my eye starting to twitch. The last time Karen had an 'epiphany', we ended up with an office slide that led straight to the first aid room.

"From now on," Karen continues, her arms outstretched like Moses parting the Red Sea, "we are an agile company. That means daily stand-ups, sticky notes everywhere, and absolutely no documentation!"

Dave, our lead developer, listens to this last point like a sheepdog that has heard the word "walk". I, on the other hand, feel like someone has just stolen my favorite pen.

No documentation? But... but... what about my beautiful 200-page requirements manifesto? Am I supposed to use it as a doorstop?

Sticky note Armageddon

Our office looks like a sticky note factory has entered into a wild partnership with a rainbow. Every wall, every desk, and even some unfortunate team members are covered in colorful squares.

Linda, our project manager, is in her element. She floats through the room like a fairy handing out sticky notes. "Okay, team! Let's have our first stand-up. Everyone grabs a sticky note and writes down what they're working on!"

We all scribble obediently on our pieces of paper as if we were primary school children doing a penal task. Brad from Marketing holds his proudly high: "Synergize cross-channel engagement for maximum user engagement!"

I'm not sure what that means, but I'm pretty sure it's not agile. It sounds more like a tongue twister for business students.

The endless stand-up

Our first "daily" stand-up takes three hours. For comparison: you could easily have driven from Munich to Berlin at this time. We ended up discussing everything from project status to Dave's new coffee machine (apparently it can brew espresso with the power of a thousand suns) to Brad's theories about extraterrestrial life.

I'm pretty sure we also discussed the meaning of life at some point, but by this point, my brain had already gone into energy-saving mode.

"Great work, team!" beams Linda as we finally finish. Her enthusiasm is as unwavering as that of a tour guide. "Same time tomorrow!"

If this is agile, please tie me to the waterfall and push me over the edge. Maybe I'll end up in a pool of sanity.

As we all stagger back to our desks, I can't help but feel like we're missing out. This doesn't feel *agile*. It feels like chaos with colorful sticky notes - like we've mistaken a child's birthday party for the project kickoff.

The secret coffee meeting

The next morning, fueled by caffeine and determination, I catch Dave at the coffee machine. I must look intense—unruly hair, wide eyes, clutching my printed Scrum Guide like it's my ticket to salvation. Last night, I wasn't able to get a wink of sleep as I was kept up by thoughts of Scrum and how I realized it was the thing we needed the most. So I decided that I would take matters into my own hands.

"Dave," I say, leaning in slightly, "have you heard of Scrum?"

Dave pauses mid-sip, giving me a curious look. "You mean apart from the shower gel?"

I shake my head. "Not that Scrum. It's a framework for managing work, especially for complex projects. It's all about breaking down tasks into smaller, manageable pieces, prioritizing what matters most, and working in short cycles called sprints."

Dave tilts his head, intrigued. "So, instead of planning everything upfront, we tackle it bit by bit?"

"Exactly," I say, warming to the topic. "A sprint is usually two weeks, and at the end, you've got something tangible to show—something that works. Plus, we get feedback early, so we're not wasting months building something no one wants."

He nods slowly, his interest growing. "And the whole team… they're involved in planning and reviewing?"

"Yep," I confirm. "The team works together to decide what's doable within the sprint. There's a daily check-in to keep everyone on the same page, and at the end, we reflect on what went well and what could be improved. It's flexible but disciplined."

Dave's expression shifts to cautious optimism. "That sounds like it could work. No more six-month marathons to nowhere."

"Exactly," I say, grinning. "It's not just efficient; it's empowering. Everyone has a voice, and the process is transparent. The Scrum Guide spells it all out, and the best part? It's free. We could start right now."

He smiles, the idea clearly taking root. "Alright, you've got my attention. Let's talk more about this."

As we head back to our desks, I can't help but feel like we're onto something transformative—a way to finally escape the chaos of traditional project management and get things done.

Unbeknownst to me, this secret meeting was just the beginning of our Scrum adventure.

Manav's Thoughts

The three-hour stand-up meeting is a classic anti-pattern. Teams often confuse having agile ceremonies with being agile. This chapter was inspired by a financial services company that had similar marathon stand-ups until we helped them understand the true purpose of the daily scrum - quick synchronization and impediment identification.

The "sticky note Armageddon" is the embodiment of the common misconception that agile means chaos with colorful tools. Brad's "synergize cross-channel engagement" note exemplifies using agile terminology without changing how we think about work and value delivery.

This is the exact journey of many teams—from skepticism ("Isn't that a bit like rugby?") to genuine curiosity about how Scrum could solve their problems. The excitement Sally and Dave share over potentially finishing something in two weeks reflects a universal desire for tangible progress over endless documentation.

Sally's initial resistance to change transforms into enthusiasm once she understands the "why" behind Scrum practices. This pattern is seen in successful transformations, resistance followed by enlightenment. The key is always finding that bridge between current pain points and Scrum's solutions, just as Sally connects her documentation struggles with Scrum's emphasis on working software and regular feedback.

The chapter ends at a crucial turning point - the moment when people start seeing Scrum not as a threat to their existing practices, but as a solution to their problems. This shift in perspective is the real beginning of successful agile transformation.

Chapter 5

The Secret Scrum

How we became Agile under the radar

Armed with my newly acquired Scrum knowledge and an amount of caffeine that would keep even an elephant awake, I decided it was time to act. In the spirit of self-organizing teams (thanks, Scrum Guide!), I've gathered a small group of rebels in the broom closet. It's me, Dave, Raj from IT, Tina from QA, and Alex from the UX team. We're crammed between shelves of cleaning supplies and towering paper stacks, like sardines in a tin can with too many dreams...

"All right, team," I whisper, channeling my inner secret agent, "we're going to give this Scrum thing a shot. But it has to stay under wraps. If Karen or Linda get wind of it…"

Dave mimes a dramatic explosion, complete with sound effects. We all nod solemnly as if he's foretold our doom.

"First off," I say, attempting a voice that radiates "I've got this," "We need to define our roles. I'll be the Product Owner."

"What does that mean?" asks Tina, sliding to the side to avoid a dangling feather duster that looks like the last remnant of an extinct species.

Clearing my throat, I summon the gravitas of a movie narrator unveiling the secrets of the universe. "As a Product Owner, I'm responsible for maximizing the value of the product and the work of the developers. A big part of that is managing the product backlog."

"Is that like our current backlog?" Alex asks, his expression resembling someone who just discovered their favorite band has broken up.

"In a way," I reply, "but instead of a dumping ground for every idea anyone has ever had, it's an organized list of everything that might be needed in the product. And here's the kicker - I'm responsible for organizing the items in the product backlog. No more random stakeholders demanding that their favorite features jump to the top of the list!"

The team's eyes light up, and I can almost see visions of a pristine, prioritized backlog swirling in their minds like constellations in a clear night sky.

"Dave," I continue, "you will be our Scrum Master."

Dave straightens up, narrowly avoiding knocking over a tower of cleaning supplies. "What's my job?"

"You are our Scrum champion," I explain. "You make sure that Scrum is understood and implemented, both within our team and in the organization. A big part of your job is to remove obstacles for the developers."

"So I'm like a project manager?" asks Dave, looking confused, looking as lost as someone trying to navigate a maze without a map.

I shake my head like a teacher correcting a wayward student. "No, it's different. You don't manage the team, you serve it. You'll coach us on self-management and cross-functional collaboration, help us focus on creating high-quality increments, and make sure all our Scrum events happen and stay within their time boxes."

A grin spreads across Dave's face, slow and sweet, like honey dripping from a spoon. "Does that mean I get to tell Linda that her three-hour stand-ups aren't Scrum-compliant?"

"Exactly," I laugh. "But maybe wait until we're out of stealth mode to do that. We don't want her throwing Gantt charts at us."

"And what about us?" asks Raj, gesturing to himself, Tina and Alex.

"You are our developers," I say. "In Scrum, the team of developers is cross-functional, which means that together you have all the skills needed to create the product increment."

"But I'm QA and Alex is UX," protests Tina. "We're not developers, except Raj."

"Scrum is not just about programming for 'developers'," I explain. "It's about creating the product. That includes testing, design, and everything else needed to deliver a 'finished' increment. You're all developers in Scrum terms."

Alex and Tina exchange glances, their skepticism melting into the kind of realization you'd expect from someone discovering they have superpowers.

"Remember," I add, "the developers are self-organizing. You decide how to turn product backlog items into valuable increments. Nobody tells you how to do your job."

"Not even you?" Alex asks skeptically.

"Not even me," I confirm. "My job is to tell you WHAT we need and WHY. Your job is to figure out HOW to do it."

The team looks both thrilled and slightly terrified. I recognize the feeling. It's like standing at the edge of a high dive for the first time—exhilarating, but with a hint of vertigo.

Secret sprinting

We decide to do a two-week "sprint" focusing on a small feature of Operation Odyssey. It feels like we're planning a secret mission, except our weapons are keyboards and whiteboards.

"Okay," I say, channeling my inner product owner, "our sprint goal is to create a working prototype of the budget tracker feature. What do you think we can achieve in two weeks?"

The team discusses, debates, and finally commits to a series of tasks. It feels... different. Collaborative. Dare I say agile?

"Remember," I add, "the Sprint is a container for all the other Scrum events. We'll have Sprint Planning, Daily Scrums, a Sprint Review, and a Sprint Retrospective, all within that two-week timebox."

"Two weeks seems so short," muses Tina, feeling like I've told her to hike in flip-flops.

"That's the point," I explain. "Short cycles mean faster feedback and more opportunities to review and adapt. What's more, no sprint is longer than a month. This prevents things from dragging on forever like a parliamentary debate on tax reforms."

The Daily Scrum Hustle

We can't hold an official Daily Scrum without arousing suspicion, so we get creative. We synchronize our coffee breaks and meet for short conversations at the snack machine as if we were a group of spies exchanging secret information in a secret rendezvous.

"What did I do yesterday? Wrote code. What am I doing today? Writing more code. Any obstacles? Yeah, this snack machine ate my Euro," Dave reports one morning as he knocks on the machine in frustration.

It's not perfect, but it works. We communicate, adapt, and actually make progress. And all under the guise of a shared addiction to stale vending machine coffee and overpriced chocolate.

The secret sprint review

Two weeks later, we have something to show for it. It's not perfect, but it works, and it's more than we've achieved in the last two months of "agile" chaos. It feels like we've just brewed Miraculix's magic potion.

We casually gather some stakeholders for a "short demo". Brad from marketing is there, along with Karen's assistant. I feel like a ringmaster about to present his biggest attraction.

While Dave demonstrates our budget tracker prototype, I watch the faces of the stakeholders. Are they... smiling? Nodding? Offering constructive feedback? It's as if someone has suddenly lowered the difficulty level of our project from "Impossible" to "Challenging".

Is that the feeling of progress? I had almost forgotten what it felt like, just like you forget what sunshine feels like after a long, German winter.

The broom closet retrospective

Back in our broom closet headquarters, we hold our sprint retrospective. The air is thick with the smell of cleaning products and success, like lemon and triumph.

"What went well?" I ask, ready to soak up any positive feedback like a sponge.

"We've actually finished something!" Tina exclaims, her voice full of astonishment.

"We got feedback before we built the whole thing," Raj adds, nodding like a bobblehead on the parcel shelf of a car.

"What could we improve?" I ask, igniting our brainstorming power.

"Maybe next time we'll meet somewhere with better ventilation," Alex suggests, eyeing the cleaning agents suspiciously, feeling the tightness of the air circulating in his lungs.

As we leave our suffocating broom closet sanctuary, there's a new bounce in our step. We may be secret scrum rebels who are a breath short after every meeting, but we're rebels with a cause - and with a potentially working product. It feels like we've just started a revolution, except our weapons are post-its and user stories.

Watch out, Operation Odyssey. The scrum team is coming to conquer you... as soon as we figure out how to explain this to Karen without getting fired. It'll probably be easier than explaining to her why we spent so much time in the broom closet.

As we scatter and try to look impartial, I can't help but feel a shiver of excitement. We're onto something here. It's messy, it's secret, it's probably against company policy.... but it works. And in the world of software development, that's nothing short of a miracle.

This Scrum revolution has only just begun, and believe me, you don't want to miss what happens next.

Manav's Thoughts

This chapter is one of the most effective, though unconventional, ways I've seen Scrum adopted - through grassroots transformation. The "broom closet Scrum" approach might seem unorthodox, but it demonstrates several key success patterns.

Sally's explanation of the Product Owner role and Dave's transition to Scrum Master show a crucial understanding that Scrum is about fundamentally different responsibilities. Many organizations stumble by treating these roles as simple replacements for existing positions.

Tina and Alex's initial resistance to being called developers, followed by their acceptance of the broader definition, reflects a common evolution in understanding. This shift from siloed specialists to collaborative developers is often one of the hardest but most rewarding transformations.

The "secret sprinting" approach offers some advantages, by starting small and under the radar, the team could focus on learning and adapting without the pressure of organizational expectations. Their first sprint's success - delivering a working prototype - validates a principle I frequently emphasize: small, focused efforts often achieve more than large, visible initiatives.

Their creative adaptation of Scrum events - like holding Daily Scrums at the coffee machine - shows it's not about following a rigid template but about embracing the principles while adapting to constraints. What's most significant is the team's reaction to delivering working software and getting stakeholder feedback. Their surprise at completing something valuable in two weeks highlights a fundamental truth: teams often don't realize how dysfunctional their current process is until they experience a better way.

This chapter shows what I call the "proof through practice" phase of transformation - where teams discover that Scrum works not through training or theory, but through actual experience. The excitement and energy they feel after their first successful sprint is something I've seen catalyze broader organizational change many times.

Chapter 6

Scrum in Secret

How our secret society saved Operation Odyssey

As our secret Scrum experiments continue, the word starts to spread. Whispers about "real progress" and "working software" echo through the open-plan offices like rumors about a new coffee machine in the canteen. Soon our storage room is no longer big enough to contain the growing group of scrum rebels.

We need a bigger space, I think, looking at our cramped space. *Or at least a conference room with fewer mops and more oxygen.*

Dave nods sagely as if he's read my mind. Our team is growing, and we carefully select new members who are fed up with the status quo and hungry for change.

Refining the product backlog

With our extended team, we take on the monster that is Operation Odyssey's requirements document. It's time to turn that doorstop into a lean, efficient product backlog.

"Okay, team," I begin, "we need to break these requirements down into manageable pieces and prioritize them by value. Imagine if we were writing a shopping list for the week's shopping, except that our budget is limited and we don't know if we'll suddenly go vegan next week."

We spend hours picking apart each requirement, turning them into user stories, and organizing them in order of importance. It's tedious work, but in the end, we have a product backlog that makes sense. We felt like we'd just cleaned out the Augean Stables, except our Hercules is a team of over-caffeinated nerds.

"I can hardly believe it," marvels Tina from QA, her eyes wide as saucers, "I understand what we're supposed to be building! It's as if someone has finally turned on the light."

I nod proudly. "That's the beauty of a well-refined product backlog. It's not just a to-do list; it's a strategic tool."

Dave looks thoughtful as he sips his now cold coffee. "How often do we do this refining thing? I mean, it feels good, but I don't want us to spend more time planning than implementing."

"That's a good question, Dave," I reply. "Refining the product backlog is an ongoing process. We'll have regular refinement sessions to break down items, add details, and estimate effort. The goal is to always have enough 'Ready' items for the next one or two sprints. It's like cooking - you prepare the ingredients before you start frying."

Alex from the UX department raises an eyebrow. "Ready? What exactly does that mean in this context?"

"Another great inquiry," I say, inwardly cheering at the team's growing interest. "For us, 'ready' means that the item is clear enough, small enough, and well understood that we could reasonably complete it in a sprint. It's part of our definition of ready. Imagine you're packing for a camping trip - every item needs to be readily packed into the backpack before you leave."

The team nods, and understanding spreads across their faces like wildfire. We have come a long way since the days of vague, novel-length requirements.

Product Backlog Refinement: It's where chaos meets order, turning vague dreams into actionable plans, and where your team learns that "As a user, I want..." is just a fancy way of saying, "Let's make this chaos make sense—one user story at a time."

Sprint planning

the art of commitment

Our sprint planning sessions developed into a master class in negotiation and estimation. Like a poker game, only instead of money, we're dealing with story points and team capacity.

As product owner, I present the highest-priority items from our product backlog. "For this sprint," I explain, my voice full of conviction, "our goal is to implement the core functionality of the budget categorization function. Here are the most important items from the product backlog that I propose for this purpose."

The developers, led by Raj, sit down together to discuss. They ask questions, break down items into tasks, and finally come up with a commitment that feels like a solemn vow.

"We think we can complete these three user stories in a sprint," Raj announces, his voice a mixture of determination and cautious optimism. "It's ambitious but doable. Like trying to eat a whole bar of chocolate without anyone noticing - challenging, but not impossible."

I nod and feel a wave of excitement that feels like the moment before the kick-off of an important soccer match. "Then let's make that our sprint goal. Remember, the sprint goal is our North Star for the next two weeks. It gives us focus and flexibility at the same time."

Sprint planning: where optimism meets reality and they somehow shake hands, like two new friends agreeing to make it work, I think as I write the sprint goal on our improvised task board.

The Daily Scrum

Stand-up Comedy

Our daily scrums become the highlight of the day. We gather in an unused meeting room, supposedly for "team bonding exercises". It feels like a mixture of secret agent meetings and improvisational theater.

Dave reports one morning "What did I do yesterday? Argued with the database. What am I doing today? Probably apologize to the database. Blocker? My incompetence,", his eyes marked by too little sleep and too much coffee.

The team laughs, but behind the humor is real work. Team members coordinate their efforts, offer help, and quickly identify obstacles. It's like adjusting an intricate clockwork mechanism, except our clockwork is made up of people, code, and the occasional tantrum.

"Remember, guys," I remind the team, "the Daily Scrum is for you. It's about synchronizing and making the plan for the next 24 hours. I'm just here to listen and note any obstacles."

The Daily Scrum: fifteen minutes of glory followed by hours of real productivity. Like an espresso for the working day - short, strong, and sometimes bitter, but it keeps you going, I reflect as we disperse for another day of coding and caffeine.

Sprint Review

Peekaboo for adults

At the end of each sprint, we hold our sprint review. It's a fine balance to present our progress without giving away our Scrum secret.

We invite key stakeholders to see our work, framed as a result of "improved teamwork and focus." Brad from Marketing joins the meeting, his eyes widen as Raj demonstrates a new feature. He's clearly impressed.

"Wow... this is exactly what I had in mind," Brad says, his tone a mix of surprise and excitement. "How did you pull this off?"

I resist the urge to smile too broadly. "Just luck, I guess. And maybe a little skill."

If only Brad knew. Our secret isn't magic, it's Scrum—and our most powerful tool is a whiteboard marker.

The feedback we get is invaluable. It helps us refine our product backlog and ensures we're moving in the right direction. We're finally speaking the same language as our stakeholders, except now our conversations are about working features, not vague promises.

Sprint Review: Where "I know it when I see it" turns into "Hey, I can actually see it!" A small victory, but one that feels like a big win for the team.

The Sprint Retrospective

Group therapy for Scrum teams

Our sprint retrospectives have become an essential space for open discussion and improvement. In our safe environment, we share our thoughts and brainstorm better ways to collaborate. It's a mix of reflection and problem-solving.

"What went well in this sprint?" I ask, marker in hand, ready to capture the team's input.

"We actually delivered working features," says Alex from UX, sounding surprised, as if this were an unexpected achievement.

"Our estimates are becoming more accurate," adds Tina, her nodding indicating approval and confidence.

"What could we improve?" The question hangs in the air, prompting thoughtful responses.

Dave clears his throat, looking thoughtful yet concerned. "I think we need to address our sprint length. Customer change requests are coming in faster than we can handle in a 2-week sprint. It feels like we're trying to outpace a bullet train with a bicycle."

We discuss the customer requests and the sprint length, and after some deliberation, we decide to keep the sprint duration for now. However, we agree on time limits for the planning, review, and retrospective meetings: two hours for planning, two hours for the review, and 90 minutes for the retrospective. It's a clear structure, designed to keep us efficient while still allowing room for collaboration.

"Remember," Dave adds, stepping into his Scrum Master role, "these times are maximum durations. We can always wrap up earlier if we've met the meeting's goal."

The team nods, feeling reassured. It feels good to shape our process to fit our needs, like adjusting the settings on a tool for a better fit.

"One last thing," I say, feeling a slight sense of unease, "we need to find a way to be more transparent. The secrecy is getting harder to manage."

We all nod, understanding the challenge. Our Scrum experiment has been successful, but it's clear that we can't keep everything behind closed doors forever. Sooner or later, the truth will come to light.

Sprint retrospectives: where old habits are questioned, and new approaches are tested. It's like a productive team discussion with fewer tears, most of the time.

As we leave our storeroom sanctuary, there's a new bounce in our step. Attention, Operation Odyssey. The Scrum team is coming - as soon as we've figured out how to explain this to Karen without getting fired. It'll probably be easier than explaining to her why we've suddenly all developed an allergy to Gantt charts.

Manav's Thoughts

This chapter illustrates the power of positive viral change - something that works remarkably well in resistant organizations.

The team's approach to product backlog refinement: converting a monolithic requirements document into a living, prioritized backlog demonstrates a fundamental shift in thinking. In my coaching experience, this transition from static documentation to dynamic backlog management often marks the true beginning of agile transformation.

Their implementation of Scrum events shows impressive maturity. The sprint planning sessions balanced optimism with reality - a crucial skill many teams struggle to develop. The daily scrums stayed focused on coordination and impediments rather than status updates. Most importantly, the sprint reviews delivered actual working software, creating those vital "aha moments" for stakeholders.

The team's handling of timeboxing deserves special attention as well. Setting clear time limits for events while staying flexible about ending early shows a deep understanding of Scrum principles. This balance between structure and flexibility often proves crucial for sustainable adoption.

What's particularly impressive is how they maintained Scrum's transparency while working "underground." Their sprint reviews cleverly demonstrated value without revealing their methods.

When Dave raised concerns about sprint length, the team didn't just react; they analyzed the situation and made an informed decision. This is how they used empirical data to make decisions. This evidence-based approach to continuous improvement is exactly what distinguishes successful Scrum implementations from superficial agile adoptions.

Most importantly, the team recognized that their "secret Scrum" approach, while effective for starting change, needed to eventually become open and official. This transition from underground movement to acknowledged practice is often the most delicate part of grassroots transformation.

This pattern of starting small, proving value, and gradually expanding influence often leads to more sustainable transformation than top-down mandates. The team's journey shows how Scrum, when properly understood and applied, naturally demonstrates its value through results.

Chapter 7

Deeper into the Scrum Waters

How we became Scrum ninjas

In the following weeks, our secret Scrum experiment begins to bear fruit. Productivity increased, morale improved and, for the first time in months, we felt like we're actually making progress.

Dave, our Scrum Master, thrives in his role. "You know," he says one day after a particularly productive Daily Scrum, "I never thought that removing obstacles could be so satisfying."

Tina, our QA expert, nods in agreement. "And the continuous integration and frequent testing makes my life so much easier."

Alex from the UX team adds: "Working closely with the developers right from the start is a real breakthrough. We're not just building features, we're designing experiences. It feels like we're finally all in the same boat - and it's no longer sinking!"

Okay, I had to admit it: we were actually getting good at this. Our "secret Scrum operation," as I'd started calling it in my head, was no longer the clumsy, awkward dance it had been at the start.

We were moving past the textbook definitions and into the messy, real-world art of it. Each sprint felt like leveling up in a video game—we'd defeat one boss (a nasty deployment bug) only to find a new, more complex challenge waiting for us (like deciphering what Mark from Marketing actually wanted).

We were refining, tweaking, and genuinely collaborating. We were becoming a real team. I was starting to feel that dangerous, unfamiliar feeling: optimism.

Of course, that's always the moment the universe decides to throw a piano at you. What we didn't know, as we patted ourselves on the back, was that our final exam was just around the corner. And it wasn't going to be an open-book test.

As our secret Scrum operation evolved, we delved deeper and deeper into the intricacies of the framework. Each sprint brought new challenges and insights that forced us to refine our understanding and implementation of Scrum. What we didn't know, however, was that our biggest test was yet to come.

The sprint that almost wasn't

How I learned to love the cancel button

In the middle of our third sprint, it happened: *disaster*. Karen, in one of her typical "visionary" moments, announced a dramatic change in business strategy. Our carefully crafted sprint goal was suddenly as irrelevant as last week's trend.

"What do we do now?" whispered Alex while I was grabbing coffee in the breakroom, his panic evident on his face. "We're only 1 week into our 2-week sprint."

I took a deep breath and remembered a passage from the Scrum Guide that I had read in one of my nightly study sessions. "Well, according to Scrum, a sprint can be canceled if the sprint goal becomes obsolete."

The team looked at me expectantly. I felt the weight of the decision on my shoulders.

"But," Dave interjected, looking thoughtful, "isn't there something in the Scrum Guide about who can cancel the sprint?"

I nodded, impressed by Dave's memory. "That's right. Only the product owner has the authority to cancel a sprint."

The team's eyes widened as they realized what this meant.

"But... you're our secret product owner," Tina whispered warily.

I straightened up and felt the full responsibility of my secret role. "Exactly. And I think... I think we need to stop this sprint."

The team collectively gasped in fear. Understandably. I have just made the decision to stop the system that we've been comfortable with for months.

"We'll use the remaining time to regroup and plan our next move in light of this new information," I continued, trying to sound more confident than I felt.

Dave nodded slowly, a grin spreading across his face. "Look at you, using your Product Owner powers. It's not an easy decision, but it's the right one."

I winked at Dave and said, "Sometimes agility means knowing when to stop and change course."

"But what about our sprint length?" asked Tina, her brow furrowed. "We're doing 2-week sprints. Are we changing that now?"

I shook my head, completely in my scrum guide mode. "One of the key aspects of Scrum is consistency. Sprints are timed events of a month or less to create consistency. A new sprint starts immediately after the previous sprint is completed. So, even if we cancel this sprint, our next one will still last 2 weeks."

"Why is this consistency so important?" Alex asked aloud as he scribbled sprint cycles in his notebook, lost in thought.

"It's about creating a rhythm," I explained, and really got going. "Consistent sprint lengths help us improve our estimation skills, make our progress more predictable, and reduce the amount of planning we have to do. It allows us to focus on the work instead of constantly adjusting our schedules."

Dave climbed in, his eyes twinkling mischievously. "Oh! It also helps with organizational alignment. Other teams and stakeholders can follow our steady rhythm and know when to expect increments and when to give their feedback. Everyone knows when to get the ball and when to pass it on."

We all nod in understanding. I felt much relieved.

"Okay, team," I said, clapping my hands, "let's officially cancel this sprint, take a day to refocus, and start our next sprint tomorrow."

I continue, "Let's use this experience to make our product backlog even more robust and flexible for future changes."

As we left the room, I felt a new appreciation for Scrum's balance between consistency and adaptability. And looking back, this experience led us to an even deeper understanding of Scrum.

The incremental epiphany

of how we discovered that we were secretly high-flyers

A few sprints later, during a particularly productive cycle, Dave walked over, his face lit up with excitement like he'd just solved a puzzle.

"Sally," he said in a low, urgent tone, "I think I've just realized something. We're actually creating multiple potentially shippable increments *within* this sprint."

I paused, letting his words sink in. "You're right," I said, recalling a line from the Scrum Guide. "Multiple increments can absolutely be created during a sprint."

Then it clicked. "And those increments? The sum gets presented at the sprint review, which ties back to how we work empirically. Technically, we could even deliver an increment to stakeholders *before* the sprint ends if we needed to."

Dave's eyes widened like the thought had opened a door he hadn't known existed. "This could totally change how we deliver value! Stakeholders don't have to wait for everything—we could get things to them faster."

"Exactly!" I replied, feeling a surge of energy. "It also highlights why our Scrum artifacts and their commitments matter so much. Let's take another look to make sure we're aligned."

I grabbed a marker and turned to the team board, feeling like a detective uncovering an important clue. I wrote:

Product Backlog – Commitment: Product Goal

Sprint Backlog – Commitment: Sprint Goal

Increment – Commitment: Definition of Done

"These commitments are crucial," I said, underlining each phrase for emphasis. "They're keeping everything transparent and focused while helping us measure our progress."

Tina looked over from her cubicle, her face bright with understanding. "So, even if we create multiple increments, every single one has to meet the Definition of Done, right?"

"Exactly," I said, nodding. "That's the beauty of it. We're not just doing more work; we're delivering more value without compromising quality."

Raj twirled his pen thoughtfully. "This shifts how I see my work. It's not about waiting until the sprint ends. We could actually deliver value several times within a sprint."

Dave grinned. "It's like we're a bakery that used to only deliver at closing time. Now, we can send out fresh rolls as soon as they're baked! Imagine how happy our customers will be."

As the team buzzed with ideas, I could see the lightbulbs going off in everyone's mind. This new understanding felt like a breakthrough, and I couldn't wait to see how it would shape our upcoming sprints.

The Scrum Purity Debate

How we learned to love the framework

As our secret Scrum implementation matured, I noticed some team members beginning to suggest tweaks to our process. It felt like watching a group of enthusiastic amateurs try to "improve" a Michelin-starred recipe.

"Do we *really* need a sprint review after every sprint?" someone asked, clearly eyeing the dwindling snack budget.

"How about we do the daily Scrum twice a week instead of every day?" suggested another, likely dreaming of a few extra minutes of sleep.

I could see the team sliding down a slippery slope—one that felt as treacherous as Everest's north face. It was time to address this head-on.

At the next retrospective, I dove in. "I know it's tempting to pick and choose parts of Scrum," I began, feeling like a stern parent about to launch into the *you-can't-have-ice-cream-for-breakfast* speech. "But Scrum isn't something you can slice and dice. The framework is meant to be implemented as a whole. If you only use bits and pieces, it's not Scrum anymore—it's just *something else*."

Some faces looked skeptical. Others were just confused. I decided to change gears.

"Imagine Scrum is like a recipe for Black Forest cake," I said, trying to channel my inner Gordon Ramsay. "You need a chocolate sponge cake, cherries, and cream. If you skip the cherries, sure, you'll make *something*—but it won't be Black Forest cake. It won't taste the same. That's exactly what happens when you only implement parts of Scrum."

The room was quiet for a moment, then a few faces lit up as understanding set in. A couple of stomachs growled.

"But here's the good news," I continued, riding the wave of enlightenment. "Scrum isn't just rigid rules—it's also a container for other techniques and practices. You *can* add things that fit our specific needs, like adding chocolate decorations to the cake. They enhance the recipe without changing its essence."

Dave perked up and jumped in. "Exactly! In our Scrum journey, using the full framework helped us spot areas where we needed extra 'spices.' But we wouldn't have realized that without starting with the original recipe."

By the end of the discussion, I could sense the team's mindset shifting. They weren't just going through the motions anymore—they were beginning to embrace Scrum's principles, using them to deliver real value.

What we didn't know, however, was that our ever-deepening understanding of Scrum would soon be put to the test. The time was approaching when we could no longer keep our Scrum revolution a secret.

Manav's Thoughts

This chapter highlights three crucial lessons for mastering Scrum: navigating disruptions, embracing incremental delivery, and upholding the framework's core principles.

The sprint cancellation scenario stands out as an example of mature Scrum thinking. The team's understanding that only the product owner should decide to cancel a sprint—not as a reaction to chaos but as a deliberate choice—reflects their deep grasp of the framework. Many organizations stumble here, either avoiding cancellations when necessary or derailing sprints haphazardly. This team, however, handled the challenge with poise, showing their commitment to consistent sprint lengths even in tough moments.

Equally transformative was their realization about delivering value incrementally within a sprint, not just at its conclusion. This shift, from "doing Scrum" to embracing empirical process control, often marks a turning point for teams. It's a mindset change that dramatically improves stakeholder satisfaction and delivery outcomes.

The chapter also touches on the perennial "Scrum purity debate." Many teams attempt to tweak Scrum before mastering it, often with disappointing results. This team's grasp of Scrum's immutability, paired with its openness to complementary practices, demonstrates nuanced thinking. Their Black Forest Cake analogy—explaining why piecemeal adoption fails—is an insight worth sharing.

Above all, the chapter emphasizes that real understanding grows through experience, not theory. By tackling challenges like sprint cancellations and customization debates, the team strengthened its appreciation for Scrum's principles. It's this hands-on learning, combined with steadfast adherence to the framework, that consistently drives the most successful transformations I've seen.

Chapter 8

The Big Scrum Coming Out

How we stepped out of the Agile closet

Six sprints into our secret Scrum operation, and the inevitable happens: Karen confronts me at the coffee machine.

"Sally," she says with a mixture of curiosity and suspicion in her voice that reminds me of a crime scene detective, "I've heard strange rumors. Something about secret meetings in storerooms and working software. Would you like to explain that to me?"

I take a deep breath. It's time to let the cat out of the bag.

The presentation of our lives

We gather the entire Operation Odyssey team and the most important stakeholders for a special presentation. Our Scrum team is at the front, as nervous as a soccer team before the penalty shoot-out, but also proud as punch.

"Ladies and gentlemen," I begin, feeling like I'm about to lift a magician's hat, "over the last three months, we've been secretly implementing a framework called Scrum."

The room is suddenly as full of murmurs like a beehive. Karen's eyebrows shoot up so high that they almost make contact with her hairline.

I start with an explanation of Scrum, its values, and how we applied it. Dave demonstrates the working features we've produced, Tina presents our improved quality metrics, and Alex introduces stakeholder feedback.

As we talk, I see how the initial skepticism in the room slowly turns to interest and finally to enthusiasm. It feels like witnessing a remarkable transformation in real-time, from something humble to something extraordinary.

The Scrum Quiz

After our presentation, the questions come flooding in, fast, and sharp.

"But how do you know what to build without a 200-page requirements document?" asks someone, looking as if he's just discovered a new truth about the world.

I explain the concept of the product backlog, emphasizing that it's a flexible list that's regularly updated and prioritized. "Think of the product backlog as a to-do list that evolves, with the most critical tasks always at the top."

"How can you plan without knowing everything from the start?" another person asks, clearly puzzled.

Dave jumps in, explaining how sprint planning helps us adjust to change while staying focused. "It's like planning a trip, but instead of having every detail set in stone, we change our route as conditions shift."

Empiricism in action: where "I don't know" becomes "Let's find out." It's like we've rediscovered the scientific method but with less formality and a lot more coffee.

The management's decision

As the Q&A session comes to an end, all eyes turn to Karen. She was as quiet as a mouse. Finally, she stands up, the tension in the room is so thick, that one can feel it with every draw of breath.

"I have to admit," she says slowly, weighing every word, "I was more skeptical at first than a psychologist at a magic show. But the results speak louder than a German dictionary. From now on, we are fully committed to Scrum!"

The room erupts in cheers as if we had just won the World Cup. Our secret Scrum team has officially arrived in the mainstream.

The Scrum journey continues

As our Scrum implementation progressed and became more integrated across the company, we encountered increasingly complex aspects of the framework. What initially felt like a straightforward process soon revealed its layers, each sprint presenting fresh challenges and offering valuable insights.

Just when I thought we were getting the hang of this Scrum thing, I realized it was like peeling an onion. The first few layers were easy—we had our daily stand-ups, we were moving sticky notes across a board, we felt productive. But the deeper we went, the more it made my eyes water.

What started as a simple set of rules quickly revealed its tricky, complicated heart. Every sprint seemed to uncover a new problem we didn't know we had, or a new "rule" that seemed to contradict the last one. Mastering Scrum, it turned out, wasn't like climbing a ladder. It was more like trying to solve a Rubik's Cube while riding a unicycle. It demanded constant learning, a healthy dose of flexibility, and the humility to accept that we were probably going to fall off a few times.

The Product Goal enlightenment

One sunny afternoon, I was sitting over our product backlog when Dave came over to me curiously, looking like a kid who had discovered that there were more levels in his favorite video game.

"Sally," he said, looking at my screen, "I've been thinking. We have all these great user stories, but what is our big goal? What are we really working towards at Operation Odyssey?"

I blinked, suddenly realizing that we had been so focused on the individual sprints that we had lost sight of our long-term goal.

"You're right, Dave," I said, a mixture of excitement and embarrassment coming over me. "We need a product goal."

I pulled up the Scrum Guide on my second monitor, feeling like I was about to discover the final piece of a complex puzzle.

"Look here," I said, pointing to a passage. "The Product Goal describes a future state of the product that serves as a goal for the Scrum team. The product goal is anchored in the product backlog, and the rest of the backlog evolves to define what will fulfill the product goal."

Dave nodded slowly, his eyes widening with understanding. "So it's our North Star for the whole product?"

"Exactly," I replied, sensing the excitement of discovery. "And another thing: the Product Goal is the long-term goal of the Scrum team. They have to fulfill or abandon one goal before they move on to the next."

We spent the next hour formulating our product goal and making sure it aligned with our company's vision and gave our team clear direction. It was as if we had finally found the lid to our puzzle box - now we could see the bigger picture we wanted to create.

The "Definition of Done" dilemma

With multiple Scrum teams continuing to work on Operation Odyssey, we noticed more and more inconsistencies in what each team considered "done". The highlight came during a joint sprint review when Team A's "completed" feature didn't fit smoothly with Team B's work.

I called an urgent meeting with all Scrum Masters and Product Owners. "Guys," I began, "we have a problem with our Definition of Done."

Tina from QA frowned. "But every team has its own Definition of Done. Isn't that okay?"

I shook my head, remembering another important point from the Scrum Guide. "Not really. If several Scrum teams are working on a product, they must jointly determine a Definition of Done and stick to it."

We spent the next few hours working out a unified Definition of Done that all the teams could agree on. It wasn't easy - almost like getting a group of chefs to agree on the perfect chili recipe - but it was necessary to ensure we were all working to the same quality standards.

The sprint backlog in-depth study

During one of our sprint planning sessions, Alex from the UX team expressed a concern. "I feel like our sprint backlog is just a list of tasks. Are we missing something?"

I paused to think about what he just said and came to the realization that we had overlooked a crucial aspect of the sprint backlog. We had made pancakes but forgotten one of the most important ingredients, the syrup.

"You're right, Alex," I said, reaching for my trusty Scrum Guide. "Let me share something important with you."

I called up the relevant section and read out loud: "The sprint backlog consists of the sprint goal (why), the selected product backlog items for the sprint (what), and an actionable plan to deliver the increment (how)."

"So it's not just about what we do, but why and how we do it?" asked Raj, his eyes shining with understanding.

"Exactly," I nodded. "And another thing: the sprint backlog is a plan made by and for the developers. It's a highly visible, up-to-date picture of the work that the developers want to do during the sprint to achieve the sprint goal."

Raj nods and off he goes.

From that point on, our sprint backlogs became much more comprehensive and meaningful. They no longer served as a simple to-do list but as a real roadmap for our work in the sprint. We had switched from a shopping list to a complete recipe.

The Scrum values in action

As we continued to refine our Scrum practices, I found myself thinking that although we were diligently following the events and artifacts of the framework, something was *still missing*.

I found this missing piece during a particularly challenging sprint when the team stuck together to overcome a major technical obstacle.

In our next retrospective, I decided to broach the subject. "Team," I began, feeling like a coach about to reveal the secret game, "I want to talk about something we haven't explicitly addressed yet: the Scrum values."

I wrote on the board:

> **Commitment, Focus, Openness, Respect, and Courage.**

"These values are the heart of Scrum," I explained, tapping each word for emphasis. "When these values are embodied by the Scrum team and the people they work with, the empirical Scrum pillars of transparency, review, and alignment come to life, which builds trust."

We spent the rest of the retrospective talking about how we had seen these values in action and how we could integrate them even more into our daily work. It was a powerful reminder that Scrum is more than just a set of practices - it's a mindset and a culture.

The ongoing journey

As I wrapped up another product backlog refinement session, I couldn't believe how far we've made it, we're not at our peak yet but we've come a long way from where we are now. From our secret beginnings in the storeroom to the transformed team we are now.

But our Scrum journey was far from over. There will always be new challenges, new insights, and new opportunities for improvement. And that was the beauty of Scrum - it provided a framework for continuous improvement and adaptation, like a never-ending upgrade of the way we work.

I felt a renewed sense of excitement. We weren't just doing Scrum anymore - we were living it, breathing it and constantly evolving, like a well-oiled machine that keeps getting better.

Who would have thought that a BA like me would end up leading an agile revolution? But then again, in the world of Scrum, anything is possible, even turning a coffee break into a productivity revolution.

Manav's Thoughts

This chapter masterfully shows the essence of successful agile transformation. The team's "show, don't tell" approach embodies what I call "transformation through demonstration." Rather than theoretical pitches, they showcased real working software and tangible improvements. This hands-on, evidence-driven strategy consistently outshines abstract talks about agile's benefits.

The questions from stakeholders about documentation and upfront planning revealed the deep roots of traditional mindsets. The team's relatable analogies—like likening the product backlog to a prioritized to-do list and sprint planning to adaptive travel—bridged the gap, making agile concepts more approachable and practical.

Their growing appreciation for the Product Goal marked an important shift. Early on, teams often focus solely on sprints, only to later grasp the importance of long-term vision. This realization, blending flexibility with direction, signals the leap from merely "doing Scrum" to truly "being agile."

The challenge of aligning multiple teams through a shared Definition of Done hit close to home. The team's recognition of its importance for product coherence reflects a deep understanding of scaled Scrum. Misaligned quality standards create integration chaos—a problem their approach skillfully avoided.

Their evolving sprint backlog approach was another standout. By moving beyond tasks to a holistic plan incorporating the why, what, and how, they unlocked a powerful tool for alignment and clarity—something I regularly emphasize.

The chapter also emphasizes the often-overlooked power of Scrum values. By embracing these principles alongside practices, the team built a foundation for sustainable agility, blending mechanics with culture.

Finally, the story captures the essence of agile transformation as a journey, not a checklist. Each insight—from Product Goals to values—built upon the last, driving continuous learning and improvement. Their evolution from quiet experimenters to organizational change agents epitomizes the most successful transformations I've witnessed: delivering results first, building trust, and fostering the adaptability needed for long-term success.

Chapter 9

Scrum Comes of Age

How we scaled without tipping over

As I sit in my regular café, sipping my latte and scrolling through the results of our latest sprint, I can't help but marvel at how far we've come. From our secret Scrum meetings in the broom cupboard to becoming a prime example of agile transformation in our company.

Our odyssey has been full of ups and downs, laughter and a few tears - and more sticky notes than I ever thought possible. But through it all, we've learned, grown, and added value in ways we couldn't have imagined in our wildest dreams.

Our successes

1. **Increasing productivity**: Our Velocity has shot through the roof like a New Year's Eve rocket. We're delivering more features in less time, and they're the features our users want. It's like we've traded in our old VW Golf for a Porsche.

2. **Improved quality**: Our Definition of Done has become our basic law of quality. Errors are detected earlier than an April Fool's joke, and our releases run smoother than a well-oiled machine.

3. **Better collaboration**: The walls between departments have come down faster than the Berlin Wall. Developers, testers, and specialist departments work together harmoniously.

4. **Stakeholder satisfaction**: Our Sprint Reviews are now more sought-after than tickets to the Burning Man. Stakeholders are as excited as if we had just brought home the World Cup trophy.

5. **Adaptability**: We change direction faster than a Formula 1 driver in the pit lane. Market changes? No problem. We inspect, adapt, and move on as if it were child's play.

The advantages of Agile

- **Transparency**: No more of the eternal "It's 90% done". Our scrum boards and burndown charts tell the truth clearer than a Swiss watch.

- **Empiricism**: We have internalized the scientific method in product development in the same way that Da Vinci internalized the art of painting. Formulating hypotheses, testing, and learning - in a continuous loop.

- **Customer focus**: Our product backlog is a love letter to our users, written with more dedication than a Shakespearean sonnet.

- **Continuous improvement**: Our retrospectives bubble over with innovations like a fountain of youth. We don't just build a product, we form a top team.

- **Risk minimization**: By delivering working increments in every sprint, we have reduced the risk of missing the target as much as a seatbelt reduces the risk of an accident.

Findings

1. **Scrum is simple, but not easy**: The Scrum Guide is shorter than a menu, but mastering Scrum is a lifelong journey like learning a martial art.

2. **Culture is the key**: introducing Scrum is more than just hanging up task boards. It's about a mindset that goes deeper than a human desire to save money.

3. **Servant leadership is a superpower**: our Scrum Masters have realized that true leadership consists of having the team's back like a good goalkeeper.

4. **Self-organization requires care**: Enabling teams to organize themselves is like planting a garden - you have to create the right conditions and then be patient.

5. **Constant learning is mandatory**: the moment we think we have mastered Scrum, we start to stumble like a skier who becomes overconfident.

The evolution of the Scrum Master

Dave's development from coder to Scrum Master is more impressive than the transformation of a caterpillar into a butterfly. He has worked his way up from a line of code to the company vision.

"Sally," Dave said to me the other day, "being a Scrum Master is like being a gardener. You don't make the plants grow, but you create a climate in which they can thrive."

My transformation from business analyst to product owner resulted in a major change of perspective. I learned that being a

Product Owner means making tough decisions like a referee in a Bundesliga final.

The road ahead

Operation Odyssey has outgrown us like a teenager. Karen, our boss, has given me a new mission: "Sally, you've done a great job with Scrum. Now we need you to explore Agile on a large scale. We need to transfer what we've learned with Scrum to the whole company."

I feel like Columbus before his great voyage - a mixture of excitement and thrill. Scaling Agile is a challenge greater than scaling Mount Everest, but if there's one thing I've learned from our Scrum journey, it's that with empiricism, inspection, and adaptation, anything is possible.

So here I am, ready for a new adventure, like a mountaineer at the foot of a still unconquered peak. From secret scrum rebel to the pioneer of scaled agility. Who knows what the future holds? But one thing is certain - it will be a ride more exciting than a rollercoaster.

Final Thoughts: The Heart of Scrum

As we conclude this chapter of our Scrum journey and look towards scaling our agile practices, it's important to revisit the core elements that make Scrum successful. These are the elements we need to preserve and reinforce as we scale:

The Scrum team: A self-organizing, cross-functional team of no more than 10 people. As we scale, we need to find ways to maintain this dynamic collaboration even as we maintain coordination across multiple teams.

The Scrum events: The rhythm of the sprints, with their planning, daily scrums, reviews, and retrospectives, is our heartbeat. Scaling will require us to synchronize this rhythm across the entire company.

The Scrum artifacts: Our product backlog, sprint backlogs, and increments provide transparency and focus. As we scale, we must ensure these artifacts remain meaningful and manageable.

The Scrum roles: The interaction between the Product Owner, Scrum Master, and developers was the key to our success. As we scale up, there will be new challenges in maintaining clear responsibilities.

Empiricism: Our commitment to transparency, verification, and adaptation has been the foundation of our ability to deal with complexity and uncertainty. This is becoming more important than ever as we scale.

The Scrum values: Commitment, courage, focus, openness, and respect have become part of our DNA. These values will be crucial in guiding us through the challenges of scaling.

As we enter the world of scaled agility, these principles will be our constant companions. The specific practices may evolve, but the heart of Scrum - its values, its empiricism, and its focus on value creation - will remain our North Star.

Off to new agile adventures!

ABOUT THE AUTHOR

Manav Agarwal is an experienced Agile Transformation Leader and Coach with a passion for making complex ideas human. With a career spanning over a decade, Manav has established himself as an innovative force in the agile community, known for implementing Scrum and SAFe® in diverse environments from aerospace to renewable energy.

With an engineer's mind and a teacher's heart, Manav's journey began at the prestigious IIT Bombay. His thinking has been shaped by international experience, including a Masters in Project Management in France and studies at the University of Toronto. This multicultural background, combined with his work at renowned companies like Airbus and Siemens, has given him a unique ability to adapt agile principles to different cultural and business contexts.

As a certified SAFe® Program Consultant (SPC) and PMI-ACP®, Manav has trained hundreds of professionals through workshops that are as entertaining as they are informative. He combines a hands-on, interactive approach with real-world anecdotes and a touch of humor—a skill he has perfected through his hobby of stand-up comedy—to make his trainings both memorable and transformative.

Manav's ultimate goal is to spread the agile mindset beyond IT, creating more adaptive, collaborative, and innovative organizations. He believes that true agility goes beyond processes and tools; it's about fostering a mindset of continuous improvement and empowering people to do their best work.

BOOKS BY THIS AUTHOR

When Sally Met Agile

Beyond Frameworks: Tailoring Agile to Your World

Join Sally on a witty and insightful journey through the messy reality of Agile adoption. Blending storytelling and practical advice, this book helps you craft an Agile approach that truly fits your team.

When Sally Met Kanban

A Journey from Chaos to Clarity

Discover Kanban through Sally's workplace adventures as she learns how flow, focus, and small changes create lasting impact. With humor and real-world lessons, this story makes Kanban approachable and fun.

The Silent Whisper

Tales of Love in the AI Era

Step into Millbrook, a small town quietly transformed by artificial intelligence. Through interconnected stories of love, loss, and humanity, this collection explores what it means to be human in the age of algorithms.

www.ingramcontent.com/pod-product-compliance
Lightning Source LLC
Chambersburg PA
CBHW070349230526
45471CB00006B/2482